THE TEARS, THE JOURNEY, THE PRAISE

A 30-Day Worship and Devotional Study Book

BY KIMELA CURTIS

The Tears, The Journey, The Praise: A 30-Day Worship and Devotional Study Book

Trilogy Christian Publishers
A Wholly Owned Subsidiary of Trinity Broadcasting Network
2442 Michelle Drive, Tustin, CA 92780

Manufactured in the United States of America
10 9 8 7 6 5 4 3 2 1
Library of Congress Cataloging-in-Publication Data is available.

ISBN: 978-1-68556-705-7
E-ISBN: 978-1-68556-706-4

Dedicated with love to my family and true friends, who prayed and encouraged me through this journey, and to all those who serve in the kingdom of God.

To God be the glory!

"Count it all joy, my brothers, when you meet trials of various kinds, for you know that the testing of your faith produces steadfastness. And let steadfastness have its full effect, that you may be perfect and complete, lacking in nothing."

— James 1:2–4

No one could have prepared me for what I was about to go through, yet God, the one and only true God, did just that.

As He molded me and shaped me through life, I had to stand alone many times with no understanding of why until now.

I thank Him, my Lord and Savior, Jesus Christ, for the preparation. For the tears that reminded me of my need for His forgiveness, love, and saving grace.

God's great love carried me through this journey of heartbreak, pain, and brokenness to a place of joy, rest, thanksgiving, and praise!

Praise His holy name, for He is my first love!

Special thanks to my husband, Ted Curtis, for the prayers, encouragement, and support in writing this thirty-day devotional journal. To my daughter, Kamela, this was a journey we took together but separate; may we both be strengthened and more like Christ each day. Thank you for the help along the way. To my son, Theo, and daughter in love, Lindsey, for your prayers, support, and encouragement! To the Holy Spirit, who guided me in writing this worship and devotional workbook. All glory belongs to You!

I pray as you go through these thirty days, you will allow yourself to be open and put down your guard. This devotional time is between you and God. He just wants you to be real with Him. When God walks through our journey with us, the tears of hurt and pain can become tears of joy, thanksgiving, and praise!

So first, let's just start with God. He knew you before you were born, and He knows everything about you already. You can't hide anything from Him or outwit Him; just be transparent with Him and yourself. If you're hurting, if you're mad, if you're lonely, whatever, just talk to Him about it. He has whatever you need.

> And my God will supply every need of yours according to his riches in glory in Christ Jesus.
>
> — Philippians 4:19

The God who gave His only Son to die so that you may have eternal life desires an intimate relationship with you. He wants to provide for you all that you need.

To take the journey and truly get the most out of it, we must start with some fundamentals.

Are you certain of your relationship with God? _____. If yes, then that's awesome. If your answer is, "I'm not sure" or "No," let's take some time and evaluate that before moving on. God wants to be a part of everything you face in life, good and bad. He's just waiting on you to invite Him into that personal space in your life. Call out to Him today, and He will respond!

the redemption that is in Christ Jesus.

— Romans 3:23–24

Because, if you confess with your mouth that Jesus is Lord and believe in your heart that God raised him from the dead, you will be saved. For with the heart one believes and is justified, and with the mouth one confesses and is saved.

— Romans 10:9–10

"For 'everyone who calls on the name of the Lord will be saved'.

—Romans 10:13

Call on Him today! He can't help you if you don't trust Him. As you go through this devotional, you will have other opportunities if you're just not ready today. My prayer is that, as you see how God has helped and guided me through the storms in my life, you will also see how my tears of pain and heartbreak became tears of praise and worship. I pray He will also shape and guide you through to a place of peace in Him and joy of worship.

Now that we have taken care of the main thing, let's move on. Oh, what great blessings we have when we belong to the kingdom of God and have confidence that He is our Father!

Are you ready to take this journey with God, ready to give it all over to Him? Start by writing out your prayer, asking God to help you to be open and receive all the truth of His Word and to strengthen you to act when led by the Spirit.

through this study. Be real and transparent!

MY PERSONAL PRAYER

_____

_____

_____

_____

_____

_____

_____

_____

_____

_____

_____

_____

_____

_____

In Jesus' name, amen!

KIMELA CURTIS

broken. I pray that through this thirty-day journey, you will find yourself closer to God and uplifted. Allow Him to work in you and through you. If you face some challenges in completing these thirty days, come back to this prayer as often as needed and remember what you're hoping to receive through your time with the Lord.

SUGGESTED WORSHIP SONGS

- "In Brokenness, I Come to You" by Christian Praise Worship
- "I Need You, God" by Consumed By Fire

Get a good night's sleep, and let's start out fresh tomorrow with an open heart to receive!

In the midst of life's day-to-day business, the thought of, *This can't be right*, kept running through my mind. Lord, how can this be? Our daughter, who has known Your Word and Your ways, identifies as homosexual. First, I was angered that she would say or think this about herself. Then I was confused; what had we done so wrong as parents? Eventually, I went to just blaming myself; maybe I was not the mother I should have been. Finally, I began questioning God. Why, God? Why would You allow this to happen to us, to her, to me? With no immediate response, I resorted to tears and heartbreak. The kind of heartbreak that only a mother can feel for her child.

I cried for days. In the morning, my pillow would be wet from the tears that I cried in my sleep. I prayed, "God, how can I get through this?" After days that seemed like weeks, I heard from the Lord, "You said you trusted in Me!"

"How can I trust You when my heart is so broken?"

"Trust Me!"

"How can I trust You when I am so confused?"

"Trust Me!"

God had to bring me back to the truth of my salvation, that being a child of God does not mean we won't face difficult situations. In these times, we must do more than say we trust God; we must *act* on the trust we have in God!

KIMELA CURTIS

faith produces steadfastness. And let steadfastness
have its full effect, that you may be perfect and complete, lacking in nothing. If any of you lacks wisdom,
let him ask God, who gives generously to all without
reproach, and it will be given to him. But let him ask
in faith, with no doubting, for the one who doubts is
like a wave of the sea that is driven and tossed by the
wind.

— James 1:2–6

THINGS TO REMEMBER
AS YOU ENTER STORMS

- Trust that God is in control
- Trust that you are not
- Trust in the bigger picture
- Trust and allow God to work in you and through
  you!

Trust in the LORD with all your heart and lean
not on your own understanding. In all your ways
acknowledge him, and he will make straight your
paths.

— Proverbs 3:5–6

- Deeper reading: James 1:1–27

when I don't really understand it or even know how to
deal with it myself.

....

This was the beginning. God was allowing me to work through all the emotions that were clouding the view of what He would have me see and the work He would have me do! But I had to be able to see the bigger picture.

....

Lord, help me to trust in Your will for my life and know
that You are working things for the greater good!

....

1. Am I open to see, accept, and respond to whatever God is exposing in my life through my situation and/or this study?

   Yes _____   No_____   Not ready _____

   Explain your answer below:

   _____

   _____

   _____

   _____

   _____

   _____

   _____

   _____

the point that I am questioning God? If not, how should I respond in a difficult situation?

_____

_____

_____

_____

_____

_____

_____

_____

3. What is clouding my view of what God is trying to reveal to me in my situation and/or through this study?

_____

_____

_____

_____

_____

_____

_____

_____

going through at this present time.

_____

_____

_____

_____

_____

_____

_____

· · · · · · · · · · · · · · · · · · · ·

*Thank You, Lord, for Your patience, love, grace, mercy,
and understanding. Your patience to let me deal with
the hurt and emotions of my broken heart. The love You
gave even in my doubt and self-pity. Your mercy to still
work in me and through me in the midst of my brokenness. For Your understanding, knowing it was time that
I needed to focus back on Your love and Your purpose. In
Jesus' name, amen!*

· · · · · · · · · · · · · · · · · · · ·

SUGGESTED WORSHIP SONG

- "Give Me Faith" by Elevation Worship

Trust in You, I hear what You're saying, God, but it's easier said than done… I'm just saying… I'm trying, with all I can, not to lose grip on what is truly taking place in my life. Prayer was and is always a priority in my life, each morning asking God to direct my path. What to say? How to respond? Not only to my daughter but also to my son, my husband, and the questions that others may have. This is a whole other side of the storm… Shaking my head… I knew, at this time, I would need others to pray for me to help keep me from falling into the dark place of self-pity! So, I called on a few of my sisters in Christ to hold me accountable to staying focused on the kingdom, to stay faithful to the Lord's will for my life… That sounds good, right? Little did I know this would be the beginning of some people being removed from my life and things removed from me. But to God be the glory! It also revealed true friendship and the truth within!

God had to show me that in the storm is when truth will come out on all sides… Okay… I have support from my husband, friends to hold me up, God's Word and prayer to keep me focused, and other believers to help me through this time in my life. I kept telling myself, "God will get me through this!" I know what you're thinking: *It all sounds like a good plan.* Well, God showed me that even when we try to do the right thing and prepare ourselves for what's to come, it may not line up with what His plan is for us.

"For my thoughts are not your thoughts, neither are your ways my ways," declares the LORD. "For as the heavens are higher than the earth, so are my ways higher than your ways and my thoughts than your thoughts."

— Isaiah 55:8–9

- God's plan will not always fit into your so-called plans (Proverbs 16:3).
- Don't fight against what God is doing in your life (Isaiah 26:3).
- God will sometimes have to remove people from your life for you to walk in His will. Some people are in your life for a season, some permanently (Ecclesiastes 3:1).
- God also will reveal and remove some things in you so you can walk in the truth, fulfilling His divine plan (Jeremiah 29:11).
- God's ultimate plan and desire is for us to do His will. When we gave our lives to Him, we died to ourselves so that He could show Himself in us and through us. Anything or anyone who gets in the way of God's plans for us may be removed.

....

Thank You, Lord, for loving me enough to continue to mold and shape me into what You would have me be.

A TIME OF CONFESSION AND PRAYER

I have found during the rough times in my life, writing down my confession and prayers first, then praying them out loud has helped me release the emotion and pain of them. So today, no questions, just write out your confessions and prayer, whatever the Lord puts on your heart, then pray about it out loud and give it to Him!

_____

_____

_____

_____

_____

_____

_____

_____

_____

_____

_____

_____

- "In Your Spirit" by Tasha Cobbs Leonard

GOD REMOVES SO HE CAN REPLACE!

God has a reason for everything that takes place in your life, including the people He places around you! Remember, some are only for a season. I won't go too deep into my experience, but only because I won't give the evil one any glory out of this. Just know that when you begin to go through the storms in your life, you must be prayerful as you move.

PRAY FOR PRAYER WARRIORS TO KEEP YOU LIFTED.

Choose them wisely. A prayer warrior does not have to know all the details in order to pray for you (Romans 15:30–32; Galatians 6:2–5). You may lose a friend or two who are only concerned about knowing the details, but that's okay; God is removing them, not you. Pray for them (Matthew 5:44–45).

STAY FOCUSED ON GOD, NOT THE STORM AROUND YOU!

If you are focused on the storm, you will miss what God is trying to teach you. (Anyone who desires to focus on the storm, let them go.) Surround yourself with those who are and will help you stay focused on God (Philippians 4:4–8)!

God can and will shine in you and through you during this time if you trust Him and surrender yourself to Him. Fellowship with those who are active in ministry work and excited about it. (Let go of those who don't see the value in serving, they don't understand God's ministry.) Remember, it is in our trials and weaknesses that God's strength and light can shine the brightest through us (1 Peter 4:10–11).

LAST BUT CERTAINLY NOT LEAST, SPEND TIME IN GOD'S WORD!

Nothing can bring you comfort more than the Word of God. Read it, listen to it, whatever is best for you. Study and meditate with God and His Word. Some may say, "It doesn't take all that," and you may lose them, but it's God removing them, not you. In order for you to hear from God, you must spend time in His Word (Romans 12:2).

Meanwhile, pray for all the people God has placed around you, even those He has removed. Pray for God's will for them; some will return, others may not! They all were in your life for a reason and a season! Trust that God knows what is best for you!

Make a list of those people God has placed in your life and pray for God's will for them physically, spiritually, mentally, and emotionally!

_____

_____

_____

_____

_____

_____

THOSE WHO HAVE
BEEN REMOVED!

_____

_____

_____

_____

_____

_____

_____

Pray for God's will and His blessing for each one. Pray for salvation if needed; only God knows!

- For His divine plan
- The person or thing may be toxic
- He has other work for you or them to do
- It is not the right relationship for you
- Everything has a time and a season

SUGGESTED WORSHIP SONG

- "Nothing He Can't Do!" by Community Music

MEN ARE FROM MARS, WOMEN ARE FROM VENUS

We did the best that we knew how to navigate through this unfamiliar territory. There was not a handbook on how to cope mentally and emotionally with understanding homosexuality with your child. We did seek advice and counseling from pastors, other believers, and family members, but none really knew what to say. Our pastor prayed for us, with us, and encouraged us to stay focused and trust God. This was also unfamiliar territory for him as well. Ted and I dealt with/handled this season of our lives differently. Long story short, it tore us apart… In hindsight, we realize there were other issues that contributed to us separating, but this was the straw that broke the camel's back. How devastating: leaders in the church, my husband being a minister, and me wearing several leaders' hats at the same time. "This will be an embarrassment to the church!" I heard this statement over and over from those we spoke to about our daughter and our separation. But I desperately wanted to share and pray with others because keeping it and trying to carry it alone was overwhelming for me.

God used this time to work on the two of us and reveal some things about our relationship that we had ignored for years. I had kept some of my deepest thoughts and opinions hidden, not knowing the impact they could and would have on our relation-

strength to make that change and that He would be glorified in my action. God answers my prayers. God desired to work in me and through me, but I had to be willing to be obedient to the Holy Spirit's direction, which was not and is not always easy.

· ·

Lord, help me to be led by the Holy Spirit
and seek to glorify You in all that I do.

· ·

Likewise the Spirit helps us in our weakness. For we do not know what to pray for as we ought, but the Spirit himself intercedes for us with groanings too deep for words. And he who searches hearts knows what is the mind of the Spirit, because the Spirit intercedes for the saints according to the will of God.

— Romans 8:26–27

- God showed me that in my weakness, He would be strong.
- Even when we don't know how or what to pray, the Holy Spirit searches our hearts and intercedes.
- When facing difficult situations, there will be times when God will remove people so that you will depend on Him and Him alone.
- Trust that God is always with you and working on you, even in the darkest of times.

according to his purpose.

— Romans 8:28

Below make a list of your weakness and for every weakness, write
a scripture showing God's strength.

MY WEAKNESS	GOD'S STRENGTHS

. . . .

*Thank You, Lord, for Your Spirit within me. For Your
strength that keeps me lifted up. Without You, I would
be lost and led astray!*

. . . .

THE TEARS, THE JOURNEY, THE PRAISE

So here I am in this unfamiliar place, not truly understanding what to do or how to do it, only that out of everyone I turned to, husband, pastor, family, friends, no one really knew what to say or how to help. So, I know I just have to wait on God to direct me. This is always a hard place to be (the waiting place).

In my waiting, God kept telling me, "It's not about *you.*" "Okay," I would say to myself, but He kept showing me that over and over, "It's not about you." Until one day, I began to think about how my daughter was feeling, my husband, son, grand-kids—how were *they* dealing with all of this? My prayers began to focus on how God could use me to help them and others. I know this sounds crazy, right? How could I help them if I can't help myself? So, I just began to focus my prayer outward and not on my hurt, my pain, my confusion, and my lack of understanding. I focused on what they may be going through—asking God to give them strength to get through this and glorify Him as well. Reaching out to each one of them had a different outcome.

First, let's talk about the relationship with my daughter, who was living a homosexual lifestyle. At this point, she was closed off, not really wanting much communication due to the fact that I was not willing to embrace the lifestyle she desired to live. Now let's get something straight, I fully embrace and love her; nothing could change that. It was her lifestyle that I did not embrace. God is not pleased with it or any other sinful lifestyle. Yes, I feel the

I didn't... Shaking my head... As a mother, all I had for her was love, and nothing would change that. So, I had to just continue to let her know I loved her and, most importantly, that God loves her. Now I know my love for her was nothing compared to the love she can have with God, so that became my focus. That was the center of my prayer for her, that she would know the true love of God, and He would be the means of her contentment and joy.

We all want to be loved and to love. I knew I had no control over that in her life. But I do know no love is as important as the *agape* love of Christ. So, if she can feel and understand that love, then the rest will take care of itself. The love of Christ is like no other!

God's love is consistent and steadfast. Despite our continual flaws, sin, and tendency to become distant from God, God's love draws us closer to Him. In a world where giving and receiving love is often conditional and fleeting, God's love is constant, stable, healing, comforting, and a source of refuge. His love is unfailing, unmovable, and unconditional. There is no love like it.

> For God so loved the world, that he gave his only
> Son, that whoever believes in him should not perish
> but have eternal life. For God did not send his Son
> into the world to condemn the world, but in order
> that the world might be saved through him.
>
> — John 3:16–17

_____

_____

_____

_____

_____

[B]ut God shows His love for us in that while we
were still sinners, Christ died for us.

— Romans 5:8

God's love is not affected by or afraid of our mess. Despite
our sin, God's love motivated and instructed Christ to die for
us so we could live in freedom from the bondage of sin. This is
amazing selfless love. This is the love I have in Christ, and this is
the love I desire for my daughter.

2. Explain how this scripture speaks to you in your everyday
   life.

_____

_____

_____

_____

_____

_____

God in Christ Jesus our Lord.

— Romans 8:39

Nothing can separate us from the love of Christ, others' love may fail, but God's love will not. His love is present through all our trials and the joys in our life.

This is a stop-and-praise-God moment! Write out a prayer thanking God for His unfailing, unmovable, and unconditional love.

_____

_____

_____

_____

_____

_____

_____

_____

_____

_____

_____

_____

_____

Amen!

SUGGESTED WORSHIP SONG

- "Your Steadfast Love" by Don Moen

YOU CAN ONLY WORK ON YOU!

Good morning, beloved. I pray your morning is off to a great start. Let's continue on from yesterday.

One of the most difficult things to do is to be transparent when you're hurting, but it also is one of the greatest opportunities to be used by God. I desperately wanted to share and pray with others because keeping the hurt and struggles I was going through and trying to carry them alone was overwhelming for me. So that's exactly what I did! Now, to be honest, in a flash, I really would prefer to leave this section out, but I'm led to include it in the hope of helping others. As I said yesterday, the thought of what others would say came and then went. I had to be concerned with what God was doing in my life and in me. I realized it was time to self-evaluate.

Now, what is God teaching me in all of this? How would I handle things spiritually, financially, emotionally, and, yes, physically? Let's start with emotions. I was a wreck on the inside, and as I began to evaluate myself, I had to spend some time with God, confessing that I didn't know how to heal the hurt, the pain, or the brokenness of all that I was facing. The Holy Spirit led me to start by reading the Book of Job. Stop here and read Job Chapter One.

also came among them. The LORD said to Satan, "From where have you come?"

Satan answered the LORD and said, "From going to and fro on the earth, and from walking up and down on it."

And the LORD said to Satan, "Have you considered my servant Job, that there is none like him on the earth, a blameless and upright man, who fears God and turns away from evil?"

Then Satan answered the LORD and said, "Does Job fear God for no reason? Have you not put a hedge around him and his house and all that he has, on every side? You have blessed the work of his hands, and his possessions have increased in the land. But stretch out your hand and touch all that he has, and he will curse you to your face."

And the LORD said to Satan, "Behold, all that he has is in your hand. Only against him do not stretch out your hand."

So, Satan went out from the presence of the LORD.

—Job 1:6–12

This was a test and opportunity for Job to honor God and show that his faith was not tied to his wealth or his blessing. Job was hurting and in pain from the loss of his family and his wealth, but he did not give up on God! Job's character and wealth were not the roots of his faith!

_____

_____

_____

_____

_____

_____

_____

_____

_____

_____

_____

Then Job arose and tore his robe and shaved his head and fell on the ground and worshiped. And he said, "Naked I came from my mother's womb, and naked shall I return. The LORD gave, and the LORD has taken away; blessed be the name of the Lord."

—Job 1:20–22

In all this, Job did not sin or charge God with wrong.

This section encouraged me to worship. Worship in my tears, my pain, my hurt. Worship the God who created me, loved me, and knew exactly what I was going through.

What makes it difficult?

_____

_____

_____

_____

_____

_____

_____

3. Name two of your favorite worship songs.

_____

_____

_____

_____

4. Name two ways you like two help others.

_____

_____

_____

_____

whatever season you are in right now, good or bad. Thank Him for it and ask for wisdom and guidance to glorify Him through it!

_____

_____

_____

_____

_____

_____

_____

_____

_____

_____

_____

_____

_____

_____

_____

_____

_____

_____

- "Nothing He Can't Do" by Community Music (ft. Meredith Andrews)

After my self-evaluation and looking in the mirror, I saw two sides of myself: first, the sinful, selfish person who was hurting and broken and wanted to be held and loved. Here I was, looking through my own eyes, with the earthly view, God standing beside me in this picture. Then, God said, "Refocus, My child." He began to remind me of the truth of all I have been given in Him. There, I saw the beloved and forgiven, a set apart servant of the Lord, the one who not only believed but had experienced His unfailing love over and over again. Here, God was holding me in His arms and His light shining through me. As believers, we know Satan will use our weaknesses to deceive us. He (Satan) wanted me to focus on my view of myself based on what I was going through. God had a bigger plan! Praise Him! Only Him! We saw it yesterday; Satan was allowed to test Job. Today, let's continue to study through Job; stop here and read Job Chapter Two.

1. What was the instruction to Satan on behalf of testing Job (Job 2:1–6)?

_____

_____

_____

_____

_____

3. Job's suffering was great, so what can we learn from chapter two, verse thirteen about our suffering (Job 2:13)?

_____

_____

_____

_____

_____

_____

Read Job chapters three through five, then let's look at them, chapter by chapter!

4. Key point in chapter three:

_____

_____

_____

_____

_____

_____

_____

_____

_____

6. Key point in chapter five:

_____

_____

_____

_____

_____

Job's faith was being tested with God's permission. He had lost everything. His wife suggested that he should curse God and die; his friend tried to comfort him, but they did not know the right thing to say or what to do (Job 42:7–8)! One friend began to point out that he needed to admit he had sinned, making Job's suffering worse. It was so overwhelming that Job cursed the day he was born. Job is being transparent, allowing us to see he has been weakened through his suffering. Satan did all he could to get Job to curse God, even using his wife to tempt him. Satan did all he could to get Job to curse God, but he did not sin against God in his words.

> "Have you not put a hedge around him and his
> house and all that he has, on every side? You have

and touch all that he has, and he will curse you to your face."

And the LORD said to Satan, "Behold, all that he has is in your hand. Only against him do not stretch out your hand."

So Satan went out from the presence of the LORD.

—Job 1:10–12

Job's faith was tested, he focused on who God was, and through his steadfastness, all was restored back to him plus some. Within ourselves, we do not have the strength to handle the suffering and trials we face. Only in Christ can we focus on who He is and know that He can carry us through. It's worship and prayer time! Today, you don't need to write it down. Just pray for your faith to be strengthened and that through any test you face, God will be glorified.

SUGGESTED WORSHIP SONG

• "Strength of My Life" by Vertical Worship

IN MY WEAKNESS, YOU ARE STRONG

Here I was in my late forties, knocking on fifty, door half-open, and I found myself in a position of starting over. Through counseling and much prayer, we agreed that physical separation would be best at the time. I had been a stay-at-home mother and wife for most of my married life, and now I had to get back out in the working world; no college degree, no working experience within the last ten or so years. I was strictly about ministry. So, I was thankful for the job I was able to get working at a fast-food restaurant, unsure of what my future held but still trusting that God was working and would provide.

Now, don't get me wrong, I was very capable of working and had worked for some years early in the marriage. But we thought it best that I stay home and not put the kids in daycare. And as they became school age, we agreed that I should be involved in their lives as much as possible—PTA, afterschool activities, football, and soccer mom. I would also take various classes, line-by-line Bible studies, computer classes, and more. We just wanted what we thought would be best for our children.

Now, I began to question if doing so was beneficial. God and I had many conversations on that matter. He would always remind me that He had a plan for my life. Meanwhile, I did my best to stay faithful to God and to my church responsibilities. There were days I felt overwhelmed and lonely, but God always made a

would come from. I prayed and shared it with a friend or two, and within days, I was able to take care of that need. Now God provided through a check from the insurance company stating that the policy had been overpaid. I had received a letter with the check in it the same day as finding out I needed the money. I did not open the mail right away, thinking it was a bill. After praying with a few people about the need, a day or two went by, and I came across the mail. Opening the mail, I just started crying and praising God for His provision. I then began sharing and praising God with a few of my sisters and brothers in Christ. How awesome, God had provided the money even before I had prayed. I just didn't know it!

God was reminding me how He had always taken care of me, and I only needed to trust Him and look for His provision in every circumstance. He reminded me that He knew my situation before I even knew there was a situation and had already provided. He reminded me that His love is like no other, not conditional but unconditional. God knew the doubt I was having in my earthly provision and how I felt like I had to do it on my own. God wanted me to see first that I could not do it on my own and second that He desired to show me His faithfulness and His provision. Jehovah Jireh, God, my provider!

....

Lord, help me to never forget
Your faithfulness and provision!

....

Read Genesis 22:1–13.

by his horns. And Abraham went and took the ram and offered it up as a burnt offering instead of his son. So Abraham called the name of that place, "The LORD will provide"; as it is said to this day, "On the mount of the LORD it shall be provided."

— Genesis 22:13–14

God has always made provision for His people (Genesis 22)!

- God provides physically, spiritually, emotionally, and financially.
- In times of need, He already knows your situation. Look for His hand at work!
- Allow God to work through others who are around you for His glory!
- Pray and praise Him from beginning to end so that others can see Him working in your situation.

1. What are you facing that you may be questioning or not sure of the outcome?

_____

_____

_____

_____

_____

_____

_____

_____

_____

_____

_____

_____

3. In what ways has God met your needs or the needs of your family in the past?

_____

_____

_____

_____

_____

_____

. . . .

Thank You, Lord, for Your provision and Your faithfulness in all situations. Your lovingkindness is overwhelming, and Your love is unconditional!

. . . .

SUGGESTED WORSHIP SONG

- "Unending Love" by Hillsong Worship

I briefly spoke of separation yesterday, so let me give some insight on that. I can only speak for myself, how I felt and how I was dealing with the situations in our lives as I began to open up to God and others about my brokenness and pain of not knowing what or how to deal with, handle, or understand homosexuality with my child. This seemed to pull Ted and me further apart from each other. In spending time with God, He showed me that this was really about trusting Him! There was no question. We both loved our daughter, and nothing would or could change that! The difficult part was understanding that I had no control over her journey, only mine. Now, don't get me wrong, I understood she is her own person, but as a mother, I wanted to protect her as any mother would.

I told you earlier that God led me to Genesis, and after reading and meditating, I knew I just had to cling to my faith and the trust I have in God, that He was in control and I only needed to look for His guidance day-to-day! In doing so, I found myself feeling stronger and stronger, but over time, I realized Ted and I spoke less and less, and he was always somewhere else physically and mentally. When he was home, his mind and thoughts were somewhere else; our conversations were less and less. The intimacy we once had was absent, and the love we showed one another was no longer there. Through conversation, counseling, and prayer, we decided to separate.

I must include this season of our lives and trust that God will get the glory (1 Peter 4:12–19)!

This was a bittersweet time for me, but it was God's time to work on me. In my time of hurting, I felt God strengthening me. His words filled my heart like never before. He showed me how He could and would use me to encourage others in similar situations, just as He had done in the past. Honestly, my heart was broken for my daughter and for my marriage, but my spirit was full of joy. There were nights I would start off in tears of brokenness and end with tears of praise! Oh, how I was thankful for this time with God alone; His molding and shaping were just what I needed.

> The word that came to Jeremiah from the LORD: "Arise, and go down to the potter's house, and there I will let you hear my words."
>
> So, I went down to the potter's house, and there he was working at his wheel. And the vessel he was making of clay was spoiled in the potter's hand, and he reworked it into another vessel, as it seemed good to the potter to do.
>
> Then the word of the LORD came to me: "O house of Israel, can I not do with you as this potter has done? declares the LORD. Behold, like the clay in the potter's hand, so are you in my hand, O house of Israel."
>
> — Jeremiah 18:1–6

_____

_____

_____

_____

_____

_____

_____

_____

2. What do you believe God wants you to see about yourself?

_____

_____

_____

_____

_____

_____

_____

_____

_____

_____

_____

_____

_____

_____

_____

_____

_____

_____

_____

_____

_____

_____

. . . .

*Thank You, Lord, for molding me and shaping me to be
more and more like You. Amen!*

. . . .

SUGGESTED WORSHIP SONG

- "Run to the Father" by Cody Carnes

JUST AS GOD MOLDS AND SHAPES US, HE ALSO PROVIDES

For the sake of this study, I will give the short version of this example of God's provision. With no college and no work experience over the past ten years, I asked myself, "What will I do?" I prayed, asking God to provide, along with asking friends to pray that God would open up a door for financial provision. I was in need and trusting that God would provide how He saw fit.

When the door opened, I accepted it. I was working at a fast-food restaurant and was thankful for the position. I remained there until the temp position opened up at the bank through a temp service. Things were going well. The position was open, and if no one applied by application closing day, I would be able to keep the temp position. I prayed, "God's will be done." On the last day, a lady from another department at the bank applied for the position, and I was let go.

Of course, I was disappointed, but I trusted that God would provide; He knew what was best, but I did not know how He was moving! Little did I know that God was already making provision earlier.

Our church secretary's mother got sick a year before, and she had to go away to take care of her. She would come home once a month to do some paperwork. Meanwhile, I would fill in with some of the work while she was away, doing what I could when I

The church trustees decided that the position needed to be filled. Now, this was taking place all while I was working at the fast-food restaurant and then the bank. The position opened up a week or so after I was let go from the bank. I was already doing some of the work... not wanting to move before God. I did not respond to the job opening. I prayed and asked God to let me know if this was the position He had for me. After a few weeks went by and prayer, I was asked to take the position. Thank You, Lord, for Your provision. Now I truly believe that if I had not trusted God as He told me, filling and helping over the past year or more, things might have been different. I went into it with confidence that this is where God wanted me to be!

God will sometimes test our faith and dependability before He places us in a position. We must trust Him even when we don't see the outcome (Psalm 66:10–12).

1. List some scriptures that encourage you to trust in God's provision.

_____

_____

_____

_____

_____

_____

_____

_____

_____

_____

_____

_____

_____

_____

_____

_____

3. List a time or situation where you have seen God's provision.

_____

_____

_____

_____

_____

_____

_____

as He provides for you as He sees fit!

_____

_____

_____

_____

_____

_____

_____

_____

_____

_____

_____

_____

_____

Thank You, in Jesus' name, amen!

SUGGESTED WORSHIP SONG

- "Spirit Lead Me" by Influence Music & Michael Ketterer

LONELINESS LEAVES ROOM FOR SATAN TO TEMPT YOU!

Here I am, clinging to the Word and prayer like never before, feeling good about how God is working in all the mess that is going on around me. Now, things began to work out for a while, and I was going about my day-to-day. Then I realized that I was just existing. I was going through the motions, and life was passing me by.

I cried out to the Lord for help. Not really knowing what it was that I really needed, but I knew God would understand even if I did not. I recall someone asking me, "What do you want?" At that time, I did not know. So, I answered that I didn't know what I wanted, just that I did not like the state I was in. I was hurt and broken and felt alone.

This was the beginning of God showing me myself in the mirror. I did not like what I saw. I saw a woman who, despite having God's love, saw herself as being unloved. A woman who had been given so many blessings. I felt everything had been taken away from me. I felt like I had lost my daughter, my husband, and my parents lived a thousand miles away from me. I was feeling alone and betrayed. Little did I know then that I was just where God wanted me to be!

As a mother and a wife, I had poured my life into my family and into others; it was and still is my nature, which made this all

was feeling betrayed, disrespected, and unloved by my husband and distant from my only son. All along, I was right where God needed me to be. It's in those lonely and quiet places that God's voice can be the clearest. There are times in life when He needs us to be in a place to see all that He is. This could be a place of trial, loneliness, and even brokenness, but it's the place where God can do His work without interruption!

"Be still and know that I am God."

— Psalm 46:10

This is not my favorite scripture; it is my *life's* scripture!

Satan was trying to come into my thoughts and interfere through what people were saying. He knew I was feeling alone, and he wanted to confuse and upset what God was doing in me. This was the time God wanted me to be about His business and not focused on my circumstances. "Being still" in the Scripture does not mean to do nothing; on the contrary, it means to get busy doing the work God has for you, placing Him before your circumstances.

Pray and ask God what it is that He would have you do. Then praise and worship Him for what He is about to do in you and through you.

How often do you take the time to just sit and worship God? Not your daily devotion, I mean a special time focused on just worshiping Him through prayer and song and maybe even dancing. I love praise dancing, a little nugget to let you get to know me better!

one. Choose a few worship songs and sing along with them as you worship Him. Allow the spirit in you to be free to worship; however, don't worry or think about anything but being in the presence of God!

1. List the things you're thankful for!

_____

_____

_____

_____

_____

_____

_____

Today, take some time and pray, asking God to help you see yourself and what He wants you to receive from Him.

2. Looking within, do you see yourself through God's eyes?

_____

_____

3. Do you allow Satan to cause you to dwell on negative thoughts about yourself and God's plan for you?

_____

_____

_____

_____

_____

_____

_____

_____

_____

_____

_____

5. Now, you know every negative needs a positive. List scriptures that tell us who we are in Christ! Here are a few to start with: Psalm 139:1; Isaiah 43:4; Galatians 2:20, 2:26; Ephesians 1:3; 1 Peter 2:9–11.

_____

_____

_____

_____

_____

_____

_____

you learned about yourself through those scriptures. Also, anything else that the Spirit brings to your mind.

> For we are his workmanship, created in Christ Jesus
> for good works, which God prepared beforehand,
> that we should walk in them.
>
> — Ephesians 2:10

SUGGESTED WORSHIP SONG

- "Make Room" by Community Music

Let me start the day off with an apology. I jumped into this as if you know who I am and how this all began. So, let me give you a little background. I am the youngest of five children, three older brothers and one older sister. My father is a pastor; he and my mother were very active in ministry and made sure we were as well. As a pastor, my father was asked to move every three to five years.

When I was twelve years old, we moved to Bluefield, West Virginia, where I met Ted Curtis, the love of my life. Yes, at twelve, I thought I was in love and was going to marry the boy I had just met. It sounds so crazy now as I write it as a woman in her fifties. But, let me just say, to make a long story short, he (Ted) is the very one I am married to today!

Ted and I were fifteen and thirteen when he first asked my father if he could come by and court me. My father told him to come back in two years. We dated off and on for five years; the first two were in school only due to the two-year mandate by my father. We got married at the young ages of twenty-one and nineteen. There were some very hard times in our journey but also very good times as well.

Now, don't get me wrong, I thought I knew what I was doing back then and had it all worked out. We both wanted to get married, Ted had already joined the military, and I would graduate and be heading to college. So we thought! We both had just

opportunity to go to the USAF's Officer Academy. Things were looking good!

Let me go back a month or two, Senior Prom. Ted came home for the weekend to take me to the prom, and he would be back off to the military the next morning. We spent as much time as possible that night and one thing led to another. Fast forward, and I was not like myself; I was feeling sick every morning; I knew something was not right… I went to the doctor's office. Yes, I was pregnant.

I'll never forget that feeling because I had never felt it before in my life. I had every emotion at one time, sadness that I would be letting down my parents, happiness, excitement that I had a life inside me, but also fear that I was not ready! I had all these questions in my head, "What am I going to do?" "How will I tell my parents?" "What about my scholarship and Olympic tryout?" "How will Ted react?" "Should I even tell him?" "Am I ready to be a mom?" So, I went home and prayed about it! The one question that never came to mind was if I would keep my child; that was not an option for me. I knew I would have this child, whether it meant I would do it alone or with help.

- God is working even when we don't see it (Exodus 3:6–9).
- How can I trust God even when I can't see Him working (Isaiah 55:8–9)?
- Deeper reading: Isaiah 55 (whole chapter)

In our difficult times, God is working the upper story through our lower story; we must remember to focus on the bigger picture!

_____

_____

_____

_____

This is very important for your walk with Christ. Write out your prayer, asking God to help you be able to stay focused on what He is doing in you, through your situation and all the things you face in life… Satan will try and keep you focused on other things

MY PERSONAL PRAYER FOR FOCUS (COLOSSIANS 3:2)!

_____

_____

_____

_____

_____

_____

_____

_____

In Jesus' name, amen!

old, I had to trust in God for His plan! He was still protecting, providing, and guiding me even when I had made mistakes. He was and is faithful in spite of our weaknesses and shortcomings.

SUGGESTED WORSHIP SONG

- "I'm Listening" by Chris McClarney (ft. Hollyn)

Yesterday was a little history about me, but I didn't give you the most important day in my life. I was thirteen years old and had been in church for as long as I could remember. I listened to the sermons, and I would even say the words with my dad sometimes as he would preach.

But this particular Sunday, we were having an evening service with a guest preacher. To be honest, I don't even remember his name, but I do remember what he said. As I was listening to him, he began to talk about knowing God on a personal level. Now I knew what the Bible said about how good God is, how He made us and everything in heaven and earth. I even knew that He died for all mankind. But he (the guest preacher) was talking about knowing Him differently, how God knew me individually and every detail about me. He said I could only know God deeply that way if I invited Him into my heart. He talked about how it was good that people went to church, but that still could not make them know God the way God wants you to know Him. So now I was really listening for some answers.

Here I was, thirteen years old and had been praying for God to answer some of my life questions. *Why was I talked about and picked on at school? Why did we have to move all the time? Why did He make me so tall and my sister so cute and petite?* You know, the silly things we worry about at thirteen. I thought maybe He was not answering because I didn't know Him like that... So, I lis-

of the sermon, but he had not given me any answers. I remember saying, "Lord, please let him say what I need to hear so I can do this differently."

Then, he began to talk about how it was important that we first believe that we are sinners in need of a Savior. That was an eye-opener at that age. I knew Christ died for our sins but never thought of myself as a sinner. So, he explained it and made it clear to me that day, and then he continued on with the full gospel. I asked Jesus into my heart that day even before he asked people to come forward.

Now, you may ask why I feel the need to tell you that at this point of the devotional. Well, for a few reasons. First, I spoke of the importance of knowing Christ in the intro but did not give you my personal testimony! Second, I do not want anyone to believe as I did that just going to church and being good would be enough... We must truly understand that just being born puts us into the sinner category, and that alone makes us in need of a Savior, "for all have sinned and fall short of the glory of God" (Romans 3:23), but the good news is that we "are justified by his grace as a gift, through the redemption that is in Christ Jesus" (Romans 3:24). Thirdly, it's important that you know God's Word tells us exactly how to ask Jesus into our hearts:

> Confess with your mouth that Jesus is Lord and
> believe in your heart that God raised Him from
> the dead, you will be saved. For with the heart one
> believes and is justified, and with the mouth one
> confesses and is saved.
>
> — Romans 10:9–10

only do that with the help of Christ. This is not about works and what you do to change in and of yourself. It's the Holy Spirit in you after receiving Christ who will help you through the changing process: sanctification!

Sanctification is defined as "the carrying on to perfection the work begun in regeneration, and it extends to the whole man."[1] It also means:

- The action of making or declaring something holy
- The action or process of being freed from sin or purified

We live our whole lives in sanctification through learning how to be obedient to the Holy Spirit. This process of sanctification takes deliberate action on our part. But first, we must call on Christ!

"For 'everyone who calls on the name of the Lord will be saved'" (Romans 10:13). I love that this scripture says "will" or "shall" be saved, *not* "might" be saved! Your part is to believe and call on Him. He and only He can do the saving and changing.

No homework today; just take the time to confirm your salvation and make sure you understand the love Christ has for you. "For God so loved the world, that he gave his only Son, that whoever believes in him should not perish but have eternal life" (John 3:16). If you have not called on Him and asked Him into your heart, do so today!

If you're sure of your salvation, just pray and thank God for His grace and mercy and love! Then spend some time in praise and worship.

- "Give Me Faith" by Elevation Worship

Tell someone your testimony today!

LET THE SPIRIT
LEAD YOU

Okay, I got you all caught up with my history. Let's get back to how God walks with us through the good and the bad times in our lives. As a mother, I have called on God for guidance for so many things, big and small. I remember when my son was in high school, and I was excited to see him mature and become a young man but also concerned about his safety and making the right decisions. Knowing I couldn't be with him all the time, I put hours into praying for him, asking God for discernment on how to guide him, when to say yes, and when to say no.

I remember one weekend, there was talk of a party coming up, and he really wanted to go. A group of guys was going to ride together; I believe it was at the lake or something. The Spirit in me was uneasy about the whole thing. I was led to tell him he could not go.

Now, you know, he asked, "Why?" He was a great student, mostly on top of his work. He was not in any type of trouble, but I was just led to say no… Yes, he was upset and did not understand. "I do my work," he said, "all my chores have been done, and I have my own money. Why?" he asked.

I remember telling him, "I know, son, but I'm just not feeling good about it."

My husband and I talked. He asked, "Why?"

Then the day after the party, I got a phone call from one of the other football moms, asking me to pray for the families of the guys in the car accident. Then, my son walks in with tears in his eyes, saying his friend got into a car accident and one of the young men lost his life. He hugged me, and all I could do was hug him back. In my mind, I was praising God for the discerning Spirit not to let him go.

I know you're thinking, *How could I praise God knowing someone's son had died?* That was not the case. My heart was breaking for him, his family, and my son, who had just lost a friend! While hugging me, my son said, "I could have been in that car." Now, I could have said a lot right there but did not at the time. The Spirit had already shown him the lesson he needed to learn! A few weeks later, we discussed the importance of being led by the Spirit and obeying His direction!

We must spend time with the Lord and be able to hear His voice and recognize His Spirit leading and guiding us. Most importantly, we must take action in obedience to what we are being led to do. I truly thought about giving in and letting him go, but the Spirit in me was so clear that I held my ground. In hindsight, I was praising God for my obedience to the Spirit. I don't know what would have happened if he had been in that car, but I do know the driver survived and was hospitalized, and one of the passengers lost his life.

Teach me to do your will, for you are my God! Let your good Spirit lead me on level ground! For your

— Psalm 143:10–11

When we listen to the guidance of the Spirit, He can and will keep us on level ground.

1. Can you think of a time in your life when you wanted to do something, but the Spirit told you to do something different? If yes, list it.

_____

_____

_____

_____

_____

_____

_____

_____

_____

_____

_____

Now, thank God for His protection!

- Deeper reading: John 16:7–15

To be led by Him, you must know Him. Call on Him today; if you're not sure, ask Him to come into your heart and be the ruler of your life!

If you're sure of your relationship but still cannot recall being led, then maybe you are not spending time with Him. Time in prayer, time in His Word, and time in fellowship with Him are a must! You are off to a great start just by going through this devotional. Now ask Him to give you the desire and longing for His Word and an intimate relationship with Him. Write it out, and then pray it out loud!

_____

_____

_____

_____

_____

_____

_____

_____

In Jesus' name, amen!

SUGGESTED WORSHIP SONG

- "Spirit Lead Me" by Michael Ketterer & Influence Music

SPIRIT LEAD ME
DAY BY DAY

Yesterday's devotion was on being led by the Spirit. I have to say, remembering all the times the Spirit led me out of some tough situation has helped me mentally. When I find myself a little down, I try to catch it at the start and begin to thank God for all the times He has directed me and guided me to respond in His will. I have learned that our mental state can be influenced by what we take in, movies, media, songs, and even what others say about us. The situation around us can also influence our state of mind.

It is so important what we do on a day-to-day basis. Personally, when things are off, I evaluate all those areas in my life. *How am I spending my time? What am I listening to? Who am I hanging with?* And, *what am I feeding my spirit?* Romans 12:2 tells us to be transformed by renewing our minds.

> I appeal to you therefore, brothers, by the mercies
> of God, to present your bodies as a living sacrifice,
> holy and acceptable to God, which is your spiritual
> worship. Do not be conformed to this world, but
> be transformed by the renewal of your mind, that
> by testing you may discern what is the will of God,
> what is good and acceptable and perfect.
>
> — Romans 12:1–2

KIMELA CURTIS

has for us. When we are in His will, living in the Spirit, being led by the Spirit, we have that inner peace and joy. Your mental state will not be based on your circumstances or other people; it will be based on your relationship with God. He wants what is good and perfect for you!

We must remember the great hope we have in Christ Jesus. The Word tells us to "think on these things" (Philippians 4:8). In all that I have gone through, with my husband, children, and even dealing with my health, it has been, still is, and always will be thinking about my hope in Christ that carries me through.

Read Philippians 4:6–9.

> [D]o not be anxious about anything, but in every-
> thing by prayer and supplication with thanksgiving
> let your requests be made known to God. And the
> peace of God, which surpasses all understanding,
> will guard your hearts and your minds in Christ
> Jesus. Finally, brothers, whatever is true, whatever is
> honorable, whatever is just, whatever is pure, what-
> ever is lovely, whatever is commendable, if there is
> any excellence, if there is anything worthy of praise,
> think about these things. What you have learned
> and received and heard and seen in me—practice
> these things, and the God of peace will be with you.
>
> — Philippians 4:6–9

Whatever you are facing, give it over to God and let Him have it. It will free you up mentally!

you believe God is requesting you to do.

_____

_____

_____

_____

_____

_____

2. Pray and thank Him for the things that you feel you are do-ing but also pray and ask Him to help you to do the things you're not doing. Call out the areas you are struggling in.

3. Read Philippians 4:6–9 again. In verse six, what two things are we told to do?

_____

_____

_____

_____

_____

4. In verse seven, it tells us the peace of God will do what?

_____

_____

_____

_____

_____

_____

_____

_____

6. According to verse nine, if we practice what we have learned and received and heard and seen, what promise do we have from God?

_____

_____

_____

_____

_____

How awesome is it that God has given us a mental checklist to keep us in check? Now don't get me wrong, I am not saying that this prevents all mental illnesses. I'm fully aware that mental illness is real, and people, even Christians, suffer from it. But what I'm saying is that the mental stress we put on ourselves by not giving things over to God can be dealt with if we practice what we have learned and received and heard and seen. If we think about things that are true, honorable, just, pure, and commendable and let Him deal with the craziness around us, we will be in a much better mental state!

COMPASSION
FOR THE LOST

Yesterday you read about the things that are pure and true. Focusing on these things helped me tremendously, especially trying to navigate through unfamiliar territory. There was so much I did not understand about homosexuality and transitioning from a secular view or spiritual view. So, trying to handle the questions and concerns from other people was way out of my comfort zone.

During this time, I would get up each morning and immediately turn on some worship music and then pray, asking God to prepare me for the day ahead. He already knew what I would be facing that very day, and I knew depending on Him would be the only way to get through it. I was so full of emotions, and I needed God to help me work through them. So as a mother, I did my research on homosexuality and being transgender through books just to get an understanding of what my baby was going through and what she may have been feeling and thinking. I wanted to have some knowledge and understanding of the terminology she was using when we spoke. I also knew it was most important to continue to study what the Word of God said about it even more.

I spoke of Genesis earlier, how we are made in the image of God. Also, in Chapter Eighteen, when Abraham interceded for Sodom, God wanted to destroy the whole city and all who were in it due to their immoral lifestyle. Chapter Nineteen is when God rescues Lot out of Sodom. The more I read through this, the

1. Stop and read through Genesis 18:16–33. What was the reason that God sent the angels to destroy the city?

_____

_____

_____

_____

_____

2. Why was Abraham pleading on behalf of Sodom and Gomorrah?

_____

_____

_____

_____

_____

You may think it remarkable Abraham even cared about the people of Sodom and Gomorrah. He could have only been concerned for his nephew and just prayed for him, "LORD, get my nephew Lot out of there first." Abraham's heart was full of sorrow and compassion, even for the wicked of Sodom and Gomorrah.

must have the same compassion and concern for others in the LGBTQ+ community and anyone else who may be lost, whomever the Lord put in my path. I needed to be open to being used for His glory!

3. Do you have compassion for others regardless of their circumstances? If not, write down the areas that you may struggle with.

_____

_____

_____

_____

_____

_____

Abraham was not looking at it from who Lot was or how the people were behaving. He was focused on God. Knowing who God is and how God works in a particular situation, he knew God to be the God of compassion who forgives. He questioned God, "Would You also destroy the righteous with the wicked?"

In asking this question, he reminded God of His own nature and principles, "Shall not the judge of all the earth do right?" Abraham thought that God, as a righteous judge, could not and would not punish the innocent in the same way as the guilty.

We must look with compassion for others and remind ourselves who God is as we pray and make ourselves available to

strengthened in our faith and confidence in who He is! Nothing is impossible for God!

I am not sure what you may be going through right now. You may be on the mountain top of life on an easy street. Either way, take this time to ask God to grow you in your compassion for the lost and other believers. Ask Him to help you see more clearly His nature and principles and have the confidence that God is fair and true!

_____

_____

_____

_____

_____

_____

_____

_____

_____

Amen!

SUGGESTED WORSHIP SONGS

- "Surely Now" by Rock City Worship
- "Nothing He Can't Do" by Community Music

DO NOT COMPROMISE

Today we will continue with Genesis. I mentioned how God would prepare me for the day, for things that I would have to face. Well, one of the hardest for me was watching the transformation of my daughter spiritually and physically, remembering the times she would ask questions about God and have a desire to talk to others about God. But I also remember when she began to question our belief in God. Now, we live in a society that believes all kinds of things about religion, Christianity, and sexuality. One question I remember vividly is, "What if you're wrong about who God is?"

I know you have heard this response, "If I'm wrong, I have nothing to lose, but if I'm right, you have everything to lose!" That was my response. Now, it sounds good, and it is true, but that in itself would not convince her or change her curiosity. So, I knew this was her way of saying she was on her own spiritual path and was looking for her own answers. All I could do was pray for her, pray for us that the Spirit would guide us through.

Shortly after, we noticed a difference in her, thinking it was the rebellious years and it would pass. We had been through it once with our son, so we put on the knee pads and would continue to pray for God's direction. As time went by, I noticed her views on sexuality were changing; society, media, songs, and even leaders began pushing these beliefs and the agenda, "We can do

society, this is now the norm, to believe you should have sex with someone to know if you are compatible with them before marriage. Along with homosexuality, being transgender, sex reassignment, and much more, all this has become the norm for this generation. We are "old school," is what we hear from her and others. The world believes we all should be accepting of it even if we do not choose it for ourselves.

Now we know there is nothing new under the sun. We saw this yesterday in our reading of Genesis. Now, let's continue with Genesis 19; this was very helpful for me. The Spirit emphasizes how Lot understood what the men wanted to do with the two guests in his house was not right, so he attempted to protect them. Lot was willing to give up his virgin daughters for the men to take advantage of to satisfy their fleshly desires. *I can't imagine what would even allow that in his thought process.*

1. Reading Genesis 19 then answers the following question: why did the men of the city want Lot to send out His two guests?

    _____

    _____

    _____

    And they called to Lot, "Where are the men who came to you tonight? Bring them out to us, that we may know them."

    — Genesis 19:5

_____

_____

_____

_____

Lot went out to the men at the entrance, shut the door after him, and said, "I beg you, my brothers, do not act so wickedly. Behold, I have two daughters who have not known any man. Let me bring them out to you, and do to them as you please. Only do nothing to these men, for they have come under the shelter of my roof."

— Genesis 19:6–9

The men of Sodom's thoughts were on pursuing pleasure; they did not see it as wicked behavior or care that Lot thought it was wicked. In Sodom and Gomorrah, it was the life they lived and saw around them. Their standards were set by those around them, not God's standards.

3. If we abandon the Bible's guide for sexual morality, what guide for sexual morality will we follow?

_____

_____

_____

"Do not think that I have come to abolish the Law
or the Prophets; I have not come to abolish them
but to fulfill them."

— Matthew 5:17

Jesus also affirmed the biblical ideal of marriage consisting
of one man and one woman joined in a life-long relationship
(Matthew 19:4–6).

4. Was God pleased with the decision for Lot to give them his
   daughters instead of the two men (Genesis 19:8–10)?

_____

_____

_____

_____

This cannot be pleasing to God or justified in any way. The
men of Sodom showed a demonstration of depravity, but we are
just as shocked at the willingness of Lot to give up his daughters
to the men as we are at the sinful desire of the men to please their
lustful desire for pleasure. Obedience is better than sacrifice (1
Samuel 15:22)!

Lot thought that through compromise, he might reach these
men, but just the opposite happened. They had no respect for him
whatsoever, even though his friendly approach led him to call
such wicked men his brethren (Genesis 19:7).

a faithful God who is always on time… God intervened, having the two men/angels save Lot by pulling him in… God is not pleased when we compromise with the world around us to fit in or be popular. We must set our standards on the Word of God!

Today is prayer time; pray that you will not compromise with this world (Romans 12:1–2). Pray that you will have the confidence to set your standards of living by the Word of God, not man.

SUGGESTED WORSHIP SONGS

- "No Compromise" by Hope's Song
- "I Speak Jesus" by Charity Gayle (ft. Steven Musso)

Continuing our lesson in Genesis, we saw that Lot was trying to prevent the men from committing what he believed to be an evil act by offering up his daughters to be abused in the same manner in which the men would have been abused. We see how Lot's moral standards had been lowered and set by men and not by God! This put Lot in a tough spot that he could not get out of on his own. The two angels/guests had to rescue him from the men of the city and from being destroyed along with the cities of Sodom and Gomorrah.

We can sometimes find ourselves in a position where we have to make some tough decisions, especially when it comes to our children. I love my daughter with all my heart, and I would not want to be the source of anything negative or hurtful in her life. Yet I have been put in some situations where I had to choose whether to offend her or offend God. As believers, we don't want to offend God, and as mothers, we don't want to hurt our children either. When we do find ourselves in that position, we must pray for guidance and help from the Spirit!

When my baby girl was born, I named her Kamela Nichole Curtis.

- Kamela: in Slavic descent, female origin, definition meaning, noble, honorable.[2]
- Through oral tradition, I was told Kamela in African descent was defined as "princess."

Now, in all honesty, at the time of choosing her name, I only knew the definition of African descent: princess, but later I looked at other definitions to see all the other attributes that had been given to the name. I had the name picked out long before I was pregnant. I would write two names in my notebook in junior high school, Theodore Edward Jr. and Kamela Nichole; it was as if I already knew I would one day have a baby boy and a girl. I tell you all this because I do believe names are important as we see so in God's Word over and over again. Now, I don't know for sure if Kamela did what she did on purpose or not, but when changing her name, she chose Melik, which is the male equivalent of Kamela (opposite sex).

- Melik: in Arabic descent, male origin, definition meaning, noble.
- Melik: in American descent, male origin, definition meaning, noble, honorable, prince.[3]

Why am I sharing all of this? First, because I was led by the Spirit to do so! Secondly, because this is one of the areas I have felt the most pressured to compromise. Family members and friends, and even other believers, asked, "Why don't you just call her by the name she wants to be called and refer to her as 'he,' if that's what she wants?" Most important is that I would rather

He created her as a female, so who am I to agree or even compromise that He, being God, should have made her a male and not female? I just can't do it.

Now, don't get me wrong, I have had many conversations with her about how hard this whole thing is for all of us. But what people don't understand is that it hurts not to give her what she wants, and it's not something I enjoy doing or even try to do on purpose… I try to just say "my baby" or "my youngest," but when I just have to say or call her name, it's Kamela or Mela, which is what we sometimes called her as she was growing up. Not to hurt her, but in honor of God, confirming I do not believe He made a mistake when He created her as a female.

Now, I know the society we live in believes otherwise. But I do not want to make the same mistake as Lot and let society cause me to compromise. I will trust God's Word and let the Holy Spirit lead me. We must remember Satan wants everything God has, and anytime he can take the glory away from God, he will try. The God I know does not make mistakes, and He gave me a daughter and a son, and all glory goes to Him alone!

1. Now today, I want you to look at your own life and evaluate it. Are there any areas where you may feel pressure to compromise or fit in?

_____

_____

_____

_____

good news is that God makes no mistakes! We can have peace in knowing that He is a perfect God who forgives us when we do fall short, but as we study His Word and draw closer to Him, we should find ourselves confessing and quickly running back to Him!

Today I just want you to look up some scriptures and write out some ways we compromise in each area.

TONGUE

For we all stumble in many ways. And if anyone does not stumble in what he says, he is a perfect man, able also to bridle his whole body...For every kind of beast and bird, of reptile and sea creature, can be tamed and has been tamed by mankind, but no human being can tame the tongue. It is a restless evil, full of deadly poison.

— James 3:2, 7–8

HIDDEN SIN

Whoever conceals his transgressions will not prosper, but he who confesses and forsakes them will obtain mercy. Blessed is the one who fears the LORD always, but whoever hardens his heart will fall into calamity.

— Proverbs 28:13–14

my sin is ever before me. Against you, you only, have I sinned and done what is evil in your sight, so that you may be justified in your words and blameless in your judgment.

— Psalm 51:2–4

2. When you read these scriptures, how do they make you feel?

_____

_____

_____

_____

_____

_____

This is the message we have heard from him and proclaim to you, that God is light, and in him is no darkness at all. If we say we have fellowship with him while we walk in darkness, we lie and do not practice the truth. But if we walk in the light, as he is in the light, we have fellowship with one another, and the blood of Jesus his Son cleanses us from all sin. If we say we have no sin, we deceive ourselves, and the truth is not in us.

— 1 John 1:5–8

for granted what we have been given, so even though we know we will fall short daily, we must allow the Spirit to lead us through this life and set our morals based on God's Word, not our society.

EXTRA SCRIPTURES

1. Genesis 11:31

   _____

   _____

   _____

   _____

2. Lamentations 3:22–25

   _____

   _____

   _____

   _____

3. Isaiah 1:18

   _____

   _____

   _____

   _____

_____

_____

_____

_____

5. Psalm 139:13–14

_____

_____

_____

_____

_____

6. 1 Timothy 4:14

_____

_____

_____

_____

_____

SUGGESTED WORSHIP SONG

- "Even at My Worst" by Blanca

One of the things that I found during this particular situation is that no one really wanted to deal with or even discuss the topic of transitioning. I believe the lack of understanding and/or not having experience in this situation made it difficult. So, most had no advice at all; others stated they really didn't know what to say but would be praying for us and with us. There really was not anyone to turn to who had walked through it, who understood our hurt, someone who could give encouragement and support, who had walked down a similar path, understanding the grief in our hearts.

For me, there was a grieving process that was taking place. When your child goes through the transitioning process, it's like a slow death, watching each stage of the process, still loving the person who is killing them, and wanting to take their place. The process is slow, physically changing in a way that's uncomfortable for them and you.

I remember the day Kamela told me she had begun the first step. Until that day, I had prayed for God to intervene. I prayed for a miracle to change her mind. Now, I was faced with how I was going to respond to what was taking place.

After hanging up the phone, I cried, then asked God to give me the strength to walk through this if it was His will to allow it. "Lord, let me be able to give You glory through it all," I said. I did

calling Ted to let him know because he was not with me when I got the call. I dialed the number, crying as I began to tell him. He said, "She started the process," and we cried together. These were not tears of hopelessness but tears of hurt and sorry for our baby girl. We knew we had a difficult journey ahead of us, an unfamiliar path that we would have to walk.

After crying, we prayed and agreed we would walk through it together. We knew this would be a time we would need to stay strong, pray up, and focus. We also knew that Satan, like a roaring lion, was lying, by the way, to discourage us in our weakest hours. We knew we could always go to each other because we understood the hurt and pain the other one was feeling. Now, remember we were still separated at this time, but God made it to where we had to depend on Him first and then each other for comfort. *Look at God...*

There were nights I was hurting, and so many thoughts of how to ease the pain came to my mind. Wine, food, sex, you know, all the things we run to that only give temporary comfort. But the Spirit in me led me to pray, and after praying, I would call the one person I knew who understood what I was feeling. There were times I would call Ted, and there were times he would call me. We cried, prayed, and there were even a few times we just sat on the phone in silence because we just knew. I'm truly thankful that even though we were having problems and not physically together, we could still talk and pray together on behalf of each other and our daughter.

Again, I saw vanity under the sun: one person who has no other, either son or brother, yet there is no

toiling and depriving myself of pleasure?" This also is vanity and an unhappy business. Two are better than one, because they have a good reward for their toil. For if they fall, one will lift up his fellow. But woe to him who is alone when he falls and has not another to lift him up! Again, if two lie together, they keep warm, but how can one keep warm alone? And though a man might prevail against one who is alone, two will withstand him—a threefold cord is not quickly broken.

— Ecclesiastes 4:7–12

We must not take for granted those who the Lord has placed in our lives; it is dangerous to completely isolate ourselves when going through difficult times. Satan will try, thinking he has an easier chance of tempting and discouraging you. Then we can easily lose focus of God and what He is doing in us and what He can do through us.

1. What can we learn from Ecclesiastes 4:9–10?

_____

_____

_____

_____

_____

_____

_____

_____

_____

_____

_____

3. Do you isolate in times of trials? Why? If not, thank God for the people that you turn to.

_____

_____

_____

_____

_____

If you don't have anyone, pray and ask God to show you someone you can turn to in times of difficulties!

SUGGESTED WORSHIP SONG

- "Surrounds Me" by Hillsong Worship

WE FACE NATURAL
TEMPTATION

Now that you have a little background, let's move forward. Now things are looking up; I'm trusting God and in a comfortable place; sounds good, right? This is sometimes a tricky time and place to be after facing difficulties. As I began to settle into this new life, feeling content, my job going well, and my stress levels down, I was able to put my guard down a little bit. That's when we are vulnerable, and Satan will use anything and everything to tempt, distract, and lure you into a place that seems safe or comfortable. But it is everything but that!

Until this point, I was so brokenhearted on every side that it really didn't matter what temptation or distraction was in my face. I was clinging to God and His Word, and that's all I could see myself doing! Now that He had begun to heal my heart and ease my pain, there was some normality in my life again.

My thoughts and mind began to wander off to my wants and physical needs. You know, I was beginning to take that second and third look at the nice-looking man who walked by. Maybe smile a little bigger when a hello came my way! You know, all those little subtle things that start off innocent. You know the feeling of being noticed across the room but not knowing who is looking. So, you look up, then comes the smile, eye contact, maybe even a little conversation. Now you go home and begin to think about that person, what they may be like, where they work?

KIMELA CURTIS

Now Satan loves to put thoughts in your mind, reminding you you're separated, you may never work things out, and this will be a start for a new relationship. The truth is we are human, and we will face this kind of temptation in life along with others. The important thing is, how will you respond?

1. Read Genesis 39. We see in verses one through six that Joseph found favor and was handsome in form and appearance. Would you say this is something Joseph earned for himself or was it given to him by God? Explain your answer.

    _____

    _____

    _____

    _____

    _____

    _____

2. In Genesis 39:7–10, the master's wife casts her eyes on him and says, "Lie with me." What is Joseph's response?

    _____

    _____

    _____

    _____

    _____

    _____

_____

_____

_____

_____

_____

4. Explain how something that starts out innocent can end up all twisted up (Genesis 39:11–18).

_____

_____

_____

_____

_____

5. Do you see any way that Joseph could have changed the outcome of being accused of misconduct with the master's wife?

_____

_____

_____

_____

_____

_____

_____

_____

_____

_____

_____

_____

7. What, if anything, can you apply to your life when facing temptation?

_____

_____

_____

_____

_____

_____

We all have natural desires that God has given us, "No temptation has overtaken you that is not common to man" (1 Corinthians 10:13).

Whenever temptation comes our way, Satan will use it to target our faith and our character and to wreck God's plan for our

high priest who is unable to sympathize with our weaknesses, but one who in every respect has been tempted as we are, yet without sin" (Hebrews 4:15).

SUGGESTED WORSHIP SONG

• "Look What You've Done" by Tasha Layton

HAVE A BATTLE PLAN
FOR TEMPTATION

YOU CANNOT BATTLE ALONE

We must arm ourselves before the battle begins. Plans fail for lack of counsel, but with many advisers, they succeed (Proverbs 15:22). Find a few trustworthy friends that you can be accountable to. Seek their advice, counsel, and prayer when needed.

WHEN FACING TEMPTATION, FLEE

We saw yesterday in Genesis 39 that Joseph fled from the master's wife. The temptation was strong; she was persistent, and she had a position over him as the master's wife. It was designed to be the temptation of all time. Yet he found the strength to flee. He found himself alone in the house where he was put in charge of all that took place. He had already found favor in the master's sight and had been given authority over all the servants. Yet he did not allow that to let him lose sight of where his blessing was coming from. It's very clear that Joseph knew that everything he had been given had come from the Lord!

> So, flee evil desires of youth and pursue righteousness, faith, love, and peace, along with those who call on the Lord out of a pure heart.
>
> — 2 Timothy 2:22

Now, we know the things we spend time looking at and pouring into ourselves have a great influence on our thinking and actions. We can either build ourselves up to be able to fight the battle, or we can set ourselves up for failure by feeding the very thing that tempts us. The psalmist said, "I will not set before my eyes anything that is worthless" (Psalm 101:3).

BE CAREFUL OF THE LITTLE THINGS; THEY BECOME BIG AS TIME GOES BY

I talked about the little things yesterday, about how they can be something innocent and feel good. But remember, the little innocent gestures can easily lead us one step at a time into active sin. Little lies will lead to more lies until you live one big lie. A little flirting can lead to cheating or to a full-out affair. Stealing a little piece of candy can become a habit that develops into stealing just for the feeling it gives you! Keep the little things in check!

> Dead flies make the perfumer's ointment give off a
> stench; so a little folly outweighs wisdom and honor.
> A wise man's heart inclines him to the right, but a
> fool's heart to the left. Even when the fool walks on
> the road, he lacks sense, and he says to everyone that
> he is a fool.
>
> — Ecclesiastes 10:1–3

We must put on the whole armor of God (Ephesians 6:11–18).

1. Write out all the pieces of the armor and what their functions are.

_____

_____

_____

_____

_____

_____

_____

_____

_____

2. Last but not least, verse eighteen tells us we must do what? When? How? With whom?

_____

_____

_____

_____

_____

Today, we, too, are tempted on every side through media, Facebook, Instagram, videos, pornography, movies, the Internet, and so many other ways. It is important that we protect ourselves and our loved ones. We have media streaming in our homes and phones all day long, and it has a great influence on our day-to-day living.

3. Take some time and evaluate your battle plan. Are you ready for battle or equipping yourself for failure?

_____

_____

4. What can you change to better equip yourself for the battle against temptation?

_____

_____

_____

_____

_____

_____

_____

_____

_____

not if but *when* you are faced with temptation.

_____

_____

_____

_____

_____

_____

_____

_____

_____

_____

SUGGESTED WORSHIP SONG

- "Promises" by I Am They

WHEN I FALL,
GOD PICKS ME UP

I pray you were able to be transparent yesterday when asked to write out your list of the things you are tempted with. The first step of overcoming anything is acknowledgment. Now I know this, I would not ask you to do anything that I have not done myself. In doing so, I had to see the true ugliness inside me, reminding me of the great need I have for the Savior.

I must say it also was empowering. Seeing your weakness also helps you find the areas where you are strong. As I prayed and asked the Holy Spirit to help me see all that needed to be revealed, the *Holy Spirit* also exposed the lies that Satan was trying to feed into my mind and spirit. Things that I have heard over and over in my life that had shaped me and were untrue were also revealed. He reminded me that I am a joint heir with Christ, and I have been given many promises. So even though I was in the midst of a separation and fumbling my way through the transitioning of my daughter and trying to understand the broken relationship with my son, I was and am still a joint heir with Christ. So, I must cling to the promises that I have been given as His child.

> For I am sure that neither death nor life, nor angels
> nor rulers, nor things present nor things to come,
> nor powers, nor height nor depth, nor anything else

1. God's love for us is certain. When reading these scriptures, how do they change the way you look at yourself regardless of your situation today?

_____

_____

_____

_____

_____

_____

At my lowest time, I was hurt, broken, and drawn in by the temptations of this world, yet God still loved me. His promises were secure; my faith in Him gave me all that I needed to overcome anything that would be set before me. I just needed to focus on Him. With the Holy Spirit's help, I prayed and asked for direction to get my heart and mind back on track, walking in His will. I was led back to my foundation, the assurance of my faith.

We have the promise of the full assurance of faith.

> [L]et us draw near with a true heart in full assurance of faith, with our hearts sprinkled clean from an evil conscience and our bodies washed with pure water. Let us hold fast the confession of our hope without wavering, for he who promised is faithful. And let

2. Read these scriptures and list all that has been given to us:
    John 5:11–13; John 5:24; Hebrews 7:25.

    _____

    _____

    _____

    _____

    _____

3. John 14:6; Matthew 7:11; Romans 8:28

    _____

    _____

    _____

    _____

    _____

4. James 1:14; 1 Corinthians 10:13

    _____

    _____

    _____

    _____

    _____

_____

_____

_____

_____

6. Romans 8:14; 1 Corinthians 2:13

_____

_____

_____

_____

_____

· · · · · · · · · · · · · · · · · · · ·

Thank You, Lord, for Your faithfulness!

· · · · · · · · · · · · · · · · · · · ·

SUGGESTED WORSHIP SONGS

- "God You Are" by We Are Messengers
- "God Turn It Around" by Church of the City

There is nothing like true worship and fellowship. Those who know me would tell you that Sunday is my favorite day of the week. I love the combination of all that usually takes place on this day. Early rise out of bed, worship, and praise as you get ready for service, then God's Word and worship with the church family. Most of the time, we go out to eat or over to someone's house with friends and family, enjoying great conversation and laughter. Then back to the house for a little relaxing time of Netflix, NBA, or a movie we've wanted to see. Maybe even a snack of two that I don't usually eat throughout the week.

The whole day just brings me peace and a sense of satisfaction. My spirit is lifted, my mind is cleared, my body is relaxed, and my whole being feels rejuvenated and ready for the week ahead, no racing about to meet a deadline, not needing to be at any certain place at a certain time. It's my preparation day. I know we can do these things every day of the week if we really want to plan it. Yet it's Sunday when all this comes together without preparation; it has an easy feel to it. I look forward to my Sundays so much; there's nothing like them.

With that being said, let me stress the importance of regular fellowship with the church family. I know without a doubt that there were Sundays when just being present in church was a great help and encouragement for me. I'm not talking about the church

want to go and didn't particularly want to see the people in the church, but I knew God had a message for me from His Word by His messenger. Remember, as a believer, there is always a message directly for you in God's Word. It may be one of encouragement, conviction, conformation, and sometimes a combination. Either way, don't let your feelings allow you to miss out on the blessing God has for you through hearing His Word and worshiping in the house of the Lord!

> Let us hold fast the confession of our hope without
> wavering, for he who promised is faithful. And let
> us consider how to stir up one another to love and
> good works, not neglecting to meet together, as is
> the habit of some, but encouraging one another, and
> all the more as you see the Day drawing near.
>
> — Hebrews 10:23–25

• Deeper readingHebrews 10:25–31

As I said, this is not about going to a building as a matter of tradition or ritual; we are no longer under the law. But it is a matter of receiving the blessing that comes with fellowship with others and also doing your part in giving back to others through our service of love. We must remember how we stood firm with God in tough, lonely, and difficult times in the past. As we remember our former days, how God brought us through, it is through Him we endured, and we are to do the same today by standing firm in our faith (Hebrews 10:35–39).

_____

_____

_____

_____

2. What will we receive after doing the will of God?

_____

_____

_____

3. What does the Word say about anyone who draws back?

_____

_____

_____

4. If we are not of those who draw back unto perdition, then what are we, according to verse 39?

_____

_____

_____

The just shall live by faith (Habakkuk 2:4; Romans 1:17; Galatians 3:11).

fellowship in God's Word with God's people to get you back on track. So, regardless of the situations in your life and even the people around you, focus on the Lord and worship the one who sustains you!

> "[E]ven to your old age I am he, and to gray hairs
> I will carry you. I have made, and I will bear; I will
> carry and will save."
>
> — Isaiah 46:4

Today our focus prayer is for our local church, for each family within the walls. Many are hurting; others may have health issues, loss of loved ones, depression, addictions, loneliness, envy, and jealousy, and there are also those who may not have relationship with the Lord.

If it helps you to write it out first, do so; if not, just pray! If you do not have a church home, pray and ask God to lead you to the place He has for you to serve, a place for you to call home.

_____

_____

_____

_____

_____

_____

_____

_____

_____

_____

_____

Amen!

SUGGESTED WORSHIP SONG

- "I Need You to Survive" by Hezekiah Walker

Yesterday, I mentioned a few things that the Spirit is leading me to address, and I will do so with His guidance, for His glory! Mainly, I stated that there were days I did not feel like going to church or even seeing the people in the church. Now, you would think, *That seems out of character for a believer.* Well, it is, but it is also reality.

In my case, going through all the different trials at that time, I was prayerful about whom I shared with. Don't get me wrong; the church knew our daughter was transitioning; they knew Ted and I were having some marital issues but did not know the details of our separation or the step by step of our daughter's process. I was not trying to hide or cover it up. I was being careful, trying not to give Satan extra ammo for his attacks.

As believers, we are still human, and people talk—and yes, they did. Things were said to me about me, and I had to always be ready to respond in a way that would glorify God, and I was not always ready to face that.

Now, can you imagine the things said and the questions that were asked? Firstly, there is a time and a place for everything if you truly care for me and about the situation. Sunday morning in the choir stand or in the hallway is not the time or the place to ask me about personal things. Secondly, if you have not called me, stopped by to check on me, or prayed with me about it, it just doesn't feel genuine to me. These are personal and private matters

or if I really want to talk with you, we have time to do so. True concern is when thought is put into the effort and the person's wellbeing is being considered!

Friendly fire hurts deeply, mostly because that's the last place you expect it to come from. So, there was a day when I woke up crying and very emotional about this journey that I was on. After days of needing encouragement but receiving questions and sly remarks about my situation, I really had to pray every Sunday morning for God to control my tongue and then quote James 3:8, asking Him to direct my response. I knew it would just take one wrong comment or question to bring me back to tears, or even worse, reply back with a sly remark of my own.

Even with the friendly fire coming my way, I was not going to miss out on my blessing of God's Word and fellowship with God's people. I was thankful that even though Ted and I were separated, we promised to walk through this together. That's exactly what we did; we prayed together weekly about all we were going through, especially about the friendly fire coming our way from other believers. Praying we would be able to show *agape* love no matter what we would face. Ted could always tell the days when I was very emotional, and I knew the days that he was also struggling. We had to give it to the Lord and be there for each other!

In doing so, we were also reminded to never forget that the church is a spiritual hospital, treatment center, and a place for all to heal. Everyone was hurting and healing in some way! When going to church, it is about our overflow of worship, thanking God for all He has done throughout the week and all the opportunities that we have been given to serve and honor Him! We had

us. Yes, my feelings were hurt at times, but nothing was going to keep me from releasing my overflow of worship! We dealt with that yesterday in Hebrews 10.

It was our blessing to receive and our opportunity to show love to our church family. You know that *agape* love. Now, just for the record, the church family consists of all believers, so when speaking of friendly fire, it came from our universal church as well as our local church family. But to God be the glory, we all are hurting and healing and growing together, so as we move through this time in our lives, some relationships are lost, but others are strengthened.

Read 1 Thessalonians 5:11–15 and answer the following questions.

1. What are we called to do as believers?

    _____

    _____

    _____

    _____

2. How are we to treat those who labor with us and over us?

    _____

    _____

    _____

    _____

    _____

_____

_____

_____

_____

4. What are we to always seek to do?

_____

_____

_____

_____

Now, I know there are times we find it difficult to walk in the Spirit, that is why we are to stay wrapped in God's Word. That is how we stay in tune with the Spirit in us. He can and will give us the direction and strength to do all that the Word directs us to do.

5. Now, read the remainder of 1 Thessalonians 5:16–28, write on the things we ought to do.

_____

_____

_____

_____

_____

_____

_____

_____

_____

_____

_____

_____

_____

_____

_____

_____

SUGGESTED WORSHIP SONGS

- "Mercy" by Elevation Worship
- "God, You're So Good" by Passion

Now I can't go through this whole devotional without spending a little time telling you about how grateful I am for those who stood strong and helped us through this journey. Not just with a kind word here and there but really sacrificing to be there. I am not talking about immediate family; they were a thousand miles away. So yes, there were phone calls with words of encouragement from time to time, but even they really did not know what to say. But God always has a ram or two in the bush. Thank You, Lord!

Firstly, let's start with our local church family. For many years I served as the youth director for our church, and I thought it important to build a close bond between the youth workers. We would have team-building exercises; we prayed together and worked through situations together as we met regularly. At the beginning of all this, I was still youth director, but by the end, my season had ended, and I was no longer the youth director. I believe a true bond was built between most of us as we served together. The youth leadership's saying was, "One team, no seams." With that being said, there was a couple I know God used for support, encouragement, and just true friendship! They were there at the beginning of the separation, all through the transitioning of our daughter, and were also a part of the accountability team. We are still great friends to this day. There were days we would meet, just

But most importantly, they recognized the days we needed encouragement the most and would act with a kind word or gesture at the right time and place, knowing the emotional state we were in. I truly believe they shared in our burdens. The time when others were distancing themselves, they remained true friends. God's Word tells us in Galatians 6:2 that we are to share one another's burdens, and that's exactly what they did. For that reason and for them, I'm grateful.

Secondly, let's talk about our universal church family. You know we all have a close circle of friends, and during this time, one of the couples just stood in the gap like never before. We did not attend the same church, but we were a part of the same family of God. No matter the time or place they were there, we cried, laughed, prayed together, and there was no better time to deepen our true friendship. There were a few times of just sitting without words, not knowing what to say but knowing that we did not want to be alone. What great love they showed to us. Now, this couple was our accountability partners also, and we were all transparent with one another. They trusted us, and we trusted them with our hurts, pain, and our weaknesses. Knowing whatever we discussed would be between God and us! We found out the hard way that's not always true with others. As the trust and bond were built between us all, we grew closer, and it made our relationship even stronger. We not only shared in one another's burden but also in our victory and life's day-to-day. Now I'm not boasting about them, but I am boasting about the God that we all serve, the one who brought us all together for this time and for His purpose. We were shown His love through them, and they made themselves available to be used by God.

help restore others. According to verses one through three, how are we to do that?

_____

_____

_____

_____

_____

_____

Sometimes as believers, we find ourselves in a place we never thought we would be, not a deliberate or planned situation, but we are there. This is when other believers have the opportunity to respond in love and help in restoration.

2. There are also warnings in passages one through ten; what are they, and why are we warned?

_____

_____

_____

_____

_____

_____

_____

_____

_____

Now, read Galatians 11–18. Remember, this is not about works that you may boast about, but with the right motive, the true love of Christ shining through you.

4. When reading these scriptures, what is the Spirit revealing to you?

_____

_____

_____

_____

_____

_____

_____

_____

Close in prayer as the Lord leads you!

SUGGESTED WORSHIP SONG

- "Available" by Elevation Worship

JUMPING AHEAD
OF GOD!

I'm sure by now you're wondering why I didn't just write a book telling you my journey from beginning to end. Well, there are several reasons, but the most important one is that I was led by the Spirit to do it this way. Honestly, this started out as a book, and I was writing it as I was going through each step. Somewhere along the way, I got busy and just stopped; that's what I told myself. I thought it was because I had so much going on and had not put aside any time to write. Truthfully, in hindsight, I believe I had jumped ahead of God, and He had to slow me down.

I truly believe that this devotional will bring Him more glory than a book just about my struggle and journey. Yes, this is about the same journey, but it also shows the application and study of scriptures that helped me overcome the difficult times during my journey. Writing it in this form allowed me to share my application of God's Word. Now, I pray it gives you the opportunity to study and apply these along with other help to your life's journey. We often jump ahead of God's plan for us; we walk in our own will. So, once I realized God wanted me to slow down, He also told me to wait. So that's what I did.

Remember Sarai in Genesis. God told Abraham they would have a child, and Sarai jumped ahead of God and sent Abraham to her servant girl.

name was Hagar. And Sarai said to Abram, "Behold now, the LORD has prevented me from bearing children. Go in to my servant; it may be that I shall obtain children by her."

And Abram listened to the voice of Sarai. So, after Abram had lived ten years in the land of Canaan, Sarai, Abram's wife, took Hagar the Egyptian, her servant, and gave her to Abram her husband as a wife. And he went in to Hagar, and she conceived.

And when she saw that she had conceived, she looked with contempt on her mistress.

— Genesis 16:1–4

1. What did Sarai do to jump ahead of God?

   _____

   _____

   _____

2. Now, read Genesis 5:16 and write out the consequences of Sarai's actions.

   _____

   _____

   _____

   _____

   _____

   _____

would do a lot of journaling as well. Later, I began to write skits and plays for my church. Then with the help of the Holy Spirit, I wrote and produced a play called "A Strong Family in a World Gone Wrong." The play ran in Oklahoma and Virginia for two nights each. Many made decisions for Christ, some rededicated, and others came forward for prayer. Later, our local church did a play called "Waging War," and I wrote that piece as well. I said all that to say, it was the Spirit leading me every time, and I knew it. I know when I'm being led by the Spirit to write and when I'm not. It was a year or two after when our family was faced with all of these challenges that I have been speaking about.

Being a person who loves to write, when I first felt that God was telling me He wanted me to write a book, I jumped in head first, not waiting on Him to tell me anything else. I just got to it, thinking it would help clear my mind from the actual day-to-day reality I was living. The flow was off, but I kept going, doing my thing, forcing the issue, but it just was not working. I knew God told me to do it but was a little confused about why it was not flowing like it used to. Then finally, I just stopped. I told myself I was too busy, and that was the excuse I used when asked, "Are you writing?" I just couldn't seem to find the time!

3. God has His way of getting our attention when we go about doing our own thing! After reading Genesis 16:5–16, how do you believe God got Sarai's attention?

   _____

   _____

   _____

She said, "I am fleeing from my mistress Sarai."

The angel of the LORD said to her, "Return to your mistress and submit to her."

— Genesis 16:8–9

God allows us to make our decisions, but He will also make sure we can't run from them. God could have allowed Hagar to flee and still protect her with promise. I believe that would have been an easy out for Sarai. He wanted Sarai to face what she had done. Remember, we will have to deal with the consequences of our actions sooner or later. For deeper reading, read Genesis 17:15–19. God had promised to establish His covenant with Abraham; he and Sarai had to be patient and trust that God would do what He promised. Are there some areas in your life where you need to wait on God? Pray and ask God for direction in waiting on Him and trusting Him in every area of your life.

SUGGESTED WORSHIP SONGS

- "Wait on You" by Elevation Worship & Maverick City

I truly want you to understand why and how this became a devotional worship study book and not just a book about my journey.

You see, the Lord wanted to use me for His purpose, not to bring glory to the journey or to the situations. Everything I am going through, many others have been through before. I nor anyone else have all the answers on how to walk through them. What I can do is share how God never left my side, how He is protecting, guiding, and healing my pain through this process.

I was jumping ahead of God, walking in my will, not His will. I had not even begun to see all that God was doing, yet I had started writing a book that I said He told me to write. So, it would have been a book about the situation, not the source of my strength during the situation. I know that writing a book about separation and all the juicy details of why and who did what might be more interesting for some. Step by step, the transitioning process of my daughter would draw the attention of others, but that's exactly what I did not want to do! I also know that is exactly what Satan wanted me to do. Satan desires to take any glory away from God; he is the father of lies and deception.

> [S]o that we would not be outwitted by Satan; for
> we are not ignorant of his designs.
>
> — 2 Corinthians 2:11

while, God was working on me, in me, and through me. He never left me; in His time, He put the words in my mind and heart to write this devotional worship study book for His glory! We must remember that Satan wants what God has! He desires to steal, kill, and destroy anything that brings glory to God.

From the very beginning, Satan has desired to be like God and have the glory that God has.

Read Ezekiel 28:12–19.

> Son of man, raise a lamentation over the king of Tyre, and say to him, Thus says the LORD GOD: "You were the signet of perfection, full of wisdom and perfect in beauty. You were in Eden, the garden of God; every precious stone was your covering, sardius, topaz, and diamond, beryl, onyx, and jasper, sapphire, emerald, and carbuncle; and crafted in gold were your settings and your engravings. On the day that you were created they were prepared. You were an anointed guardian cherub. I placed you; you were on the holy mountain of God; in the midst of the stones of fire you walked. You were blameless in your ways from the day you were created, till unrighteousness was found in you. In the abundance of your trade you were filled with violence in your midst, and you sinned; so I cast you as a profane thing from the mountain of God, and I destroyed you, O guardian cherub, from the midst of the stones of fire. Your heart was proud because of your beauty; you corrupted your wisdom for the sake of

multitude of your iniquities, in the unrighteousness of your trade you profaned your sanctuaries; so I brought fire out from your midst; it consumed you, and I turned you to ashes on the earth in the sight of all who saw you. All who know you among the peoples are appalled at you; you have come to a dreadful end and shall be no more forever."

— Ezekiel 28:12–19

How you are fallen from heaven, O Day Star, son of Dawn! How you are cut down to the ground, you who laid the nations low! You said in your heart, "I will ascend to heaven; above the stars of God, I will set my throne on high; I will sit on the mount of assembly in the far reaches of the north; I will ascend above the heights of the clouds; I will make myself like the Most High."

— Isaiah 14:12–14

1. List all the *I wills* in this passage.

    I will_____.

    I will_____.

    I will_____.

    I will_____.

    I will_____.

When we walk in our own will, we are rejecting God's will for our life. Doing things our way takes the glory away from God!

And the great dragon was thrown down, that ancient serpent, who is called the devil and Satan, the deceiver of the whole world—he was thrown down to the earth, and his angels were thrown down with him.

— Revelation 12:9

Satan has been crafty and deceitful from the beginning.

Now the serpent was more crafty than any other beast of the field that the LORD God had made. He said to the woman, "Did God actually say, 'You shall not eat of any tree in the garden'?"

And the woman said to the serpent, "We may eat of the fruit of the trees in the garden, but God said, 'You shall not eat of the fruit of the tree that is in the midst of the garden, neither shall you touch it, lest you die.'"

But the serpent said to the woman, "You will not surely die."

— Genesis 3:1–4

Don't let Satan fool you with his tricks, be on guard, watchful of his schemes; he will try to disrupt what God is doing in your life! Pray for wisdom to know when Satan is attacking you and that you will submit to God!

- "God, Turn It Around" by Jon Reddick

Today will be difficult for me, but I will get through it with the help of the Lord and the guidance of the Holy Spirit. You can't know what it's like to be a mother unless you are a mother.

I say that because no one could understand how I was feeling or what I was going through as my daughter was transitioning. I was the one who carried her for nine months, the only one who tried to breastfeed her, who stayed up all night when she had colic. The one who searched every store in the city for the Suzy Cute doll she just had to have for Christmas. The one who wiped her tears when a boy had broken her heart. She is my baby girl. I would not change a minute of it.

That's why it was so hard watching this take place; with each step, I felt like I was losing my baby girl. Each time, I would see something was different about her. Just as I had seen a spiritual change, now I was seeing a physical change right before my eyes. I had to be careful not to lose sight of what God was doing in me.

I remember the time I was meeting her for dinner in Tulsa. We were to meet at a place I had never been to before. She said, "I will meet you outside," I guess so I would not miss it. I drove up and looked for her and did not see her, so I parked and waited a little while. Then I called her phone to make sure I was at the right place. She said, "I am standing outside the door."

So, I looked up at the door and saw the young man that was there when I pulled up but did not see her. Then I realized that it

my tears and then went to meet her.

Now, this was another bittersweet moment for me. Spending time with my children has always been a blessing for me, something I look forward to, but this was becoming difficult to navigate. I found myself needing to pray about the uneasy feeling of not knowing what changes I would see each time we met. It was just hard, to say the least.

Afterward, I remember calling one of my closest girlfriends. Yes, crying again because of all the changes; I felt like I was losing my baby. Not only was her appearance changing, but she sounded different, and it was just difficult to hold it together.

My friend listened, then said to me, "Kim, you wanted to see her, right?"

I said, "Yes."

She said, "Well, you did." Then she asked, "Did you guys talk about the things you wanted to?"

I said, "Yes."

She said, "That's good." Then she reminded me of something I said to her a while back, "Remember you told me 'as long as she is breathing, God is not finished'?"

I said, "You're right." That's exactly what I needed to hear. God is still at work. Just as God is not finished with me, He is not finished with any of us.

> And I am sure of this, that he who began a good
> work in you will bring it to completion at the day of
> Jesus Christ.

> — Philippians 1:6

in being able to be with her, touch her, and communicate with her. Christians sometimes are stereotyped as people who disown their own family when it comes to homosexuality and transitioning, but that is such an untruth. In the process, a lot happens, and it may look like that from the outside, but until you walk through this situation, you will never understand.

This was difficult on both sides, and there were times when she did not want to see us. I understood that and wanted nothing but to be there for my child. I loved her and always will, but just like any parent, I was not pleased with her lifestyle. But I was not going to give Satan room to be deceitful, crafty, and try to destroy the relationship with my child, my baby girl. I committed after that day that I would be prayerful of his tricky schemes and be mindful that his future is already determined and the battle is already won.

It is important for us to know that Satan is real, and he desires to destroy mankind.

> Be sober-minded; be watchful. Your adversary the
> devil prowls around like a roaring lion, seeking
> someone to devour.
>
> — 1 Peter 5:8

1. Take this time to write out any area of your life where Satan may be trying to deceive you.

_____

_____

Remember that:

- Satan is a liar and a murderer (John 8:39–47).
- God is truth and the way to life (John 14:6–14).
- Satan has been given authority in the world (1 John 2:15–16; Ephesians 6:12–13; Luke 4:5–12).
- God is the Most High ruler over the realm of mankind (Daniel 4:17; Mark 1:27).

2. Why must we understand Satan's plan (2 Corinthians 2:11)?

_____

_____

_____

_____

_____

3. What should we do in order for Satan to flee (James 4:6–7)?

_____

_____

_____

_____

_____

The LORD brings the counsel of the nations to nothing; he frustrates the plans of the peoples. The counsel of the LORD stands forever, the plans of his heart to all generations. Blessed is the nation whose God is the LORD, the people whom he has chosen as his heritage! The LORD looks down from heaven; he sees all the children of man; from where he sits enthroned he looks out on all the inhabitants of the earth, he who fashions the hearts of them all and observes all their deeds. The king is not saved by his great army; a warrior is not delivered by his great strength. The war horse is a false hope for salvation, and by its great might it cannot rescue. Behold, the eye of the LORD is on those who fear him, on those who hope in his steadfast love, that he may deliver their soul from death and keep them alive in famine. Our soul waits for the LORD; he is our help and our shield. For our heart is glad in him, because we trust in his holy name. Let your steadfast love, O LORD, be upon us, even as we hope in you.

— Psalm 33:10–22

Satan has already been defeated when Christ died on the cross and rose again; He made the devil powerless.

Since therefore the children share in flesh and blood, he himself likewise partook of the same things, that

those who through fear of death were subject to life-long slavery. For surely it is not angels that he helps, but he helps the offspring of Abraham.

— Hebrews 2:14–16

4. Who destroyed the one who had the power of death?

_____

_____

5. Who had the power of death?

_____

_____

6. What are we free from?

_____

_____

_____

_____

_____

7. Who is this freedom for?

_____

_____

_____

_____

_____

seeking to destroy anything that brings glory to God! Even with something as small as a devotional book, Satan will try and destroy it. But when we submit ourselves to God, resist the devil, and do things in God's will and not our own, God will take care of the rest, and Satan will have to flee. Remember, Satan is already defeated!

SUGGESTED WORSHIP SONGS

- "See a Victory" by Elevation Worship
- "None but Jesus" by Brooke Fraser

THROUGH CHRIST WHO STRENGTHENS ME

Now, I know many people have been through a separation. I don't know anyone personally who has gone through a family member transitioning. Believe me, this is not an easy road to travel down. I also know it seems to be a topic that believers are not comfortable dealing with, which makes it more difficult for us. I pray that through our experience, we will be able to help others who may find themselves in this situation.

We found ourselves taking refuge with God, who is our main source of strength. I truly believe the things we go through in life are for God's glory, and I don't know what the Lord will do through all of this, but I do know that I am available to be used how He sees fit to use me. We have already been called on to talk with others and share with others throughout this journey. It has helped to strengthen us and grow us. I'm praising God for the strength that He has given me thus far, for His love and His confidence in me to trust Him. The Word tells us that we have our strength in Christ Jesus.

— Philippians 4:13,
clarification in brackets is added by the author

I truly believe Christ will not only get us through this but that He will get the glory in the end!

You guide me with your counsel, and afterward you will receive me to glory.

— Psalm 73:24

. . . .

Lord, help me to always run to You when my heart and mind are heavy; may Your presents be my place of refuge.

. . . .

The LORD is my strength and my shield; in him my heart trusts, and I am helped; my heart exults, and with my song I give thanks to him. The LORD is the strength of his people; he is the saving refuge of his anointed.

— Psalm 28:7–8

Whom have I in heaven but you? And there is nothing on earth that I desire besides you. My flesh and my heart may fail, but God is the strength of my heart and my portion forever. For behold, those

good to be near God; I have made the Lord GOD my refuge, that I may tell of all your works.

— Psalm 73:25–28

Read the entire chapter (Psalm 73) for extra reading!

1. How can we find refuge in Christ?

_____

_____

_____

_____

2. How do you prioritize your time spent in prayer and the study of God's Word?

_____

_____

_____

_____

3. What improvements can you make?

_____

_____

_____

_____

_____

_____

_____

_____

_____

_____

_____

_____

_____

_____

_____

_____

_____

_____

_____

5. Do you find it hard to give thanks to God during a difficult time in your life?

_____

_____

_____

_____

_____

_____

_____

_____

_____

_____

_____

_____

_____

_____

_____

_____

_____

. . . .

Lord, thank You for always being near to me and
providing me that peaceful place to run and find rest
in Your presents. Thank You for Your promise to be my
strength, my shield, and my refuge.

. . . .

SUGGESTED WORSHIP SONGS

- "You Have Made Me Glad" by Charity Gayle
- "Gratitude" by Brandon Lake

KIMELA CURTIS

Here we are at day thirty, and I pray you've been helped and encouraged. Remember, as believers, we will face all kinds of trials and tribulations. We are being tested in our faith and strengthened in our faithfulness. We must stand firm in the truth and have compassion for others.

As I write the last day of this devotional, I must say things are better.

Ted and I had to walk through this time of separation and the process of our daughter transitioning in our own separate ways, which were different for each of us. Yet we still were there for one another. We prayed together, cried together, and we even worshipped together all the way through. Now, God has seen fit to bring us back together. We are still working through some things in our marriage, and we will until we go see Jesus.

My relationship with my son has been mended, and we know Satan tried to use life's situations to cloud our love for one another as mother and son.

Last but certainly not least, Kamela and I continue to grow through this process. But our love for one another is strong. Yes, she is transgender and goes by the name Melik, but she will always be my baby girl. I love her, but God loves her more.

Through all of this, I pray that you see that we must let God handle His business and just be obedient to what He asks of us!

the victory is His, and we have to live in that victory that we have been given.

I truly believe that every believer should read through Revelation at least once a year. It's not as difficult as some believe. The word "revelation" means "the revealing divine truth of Christ Jesus." That divine truth is our victory—the victory of what we have through, salvation in Christ, the victory of hope in Christ, the victory of eternal life in heaven with Christ. The Book of Revelation tells us that in the final battle, the enemy will be defeated before the battle even starts because it's already done! I know many people try to stay away from Revelation, but the more I read it, the more it is closer to the top of my list of favorites. You see, it's a book of hope for the believer. Satan does not want you to understand that because our victory is his—*Satan's*—*defeat* and of all who follow him.

Revelation starts out with a blessing for believers; we are told in Chapter One that those who read, hear, and keep it will be blessed.

> Blessed is the one who reads aloud the words of this prophecy, and blessed are those who hear, and who keep what is written in it, for the time is near.
>
> — Revelation 1:3

This message was from God, who gave it to Jesus, who gave it to the angels, who then gave it to the servants to take to the churches (Revelation 1:1–2). So we know it is for us, yet we really don't hear much preaching or teaching in this book. I challenge

churches. Yet the messages are applicable for today! Today, we are just taking a little glean through it. My prayer is that you will take the time to read through its entirety. Ask the Holy Spirit to reveal the truth and all its great hopes for believers. I just want you to see the great hope that you can have through Chapter Twenty. No matter what we face and how hard Satan tries to defeat us, he will never have victory over the believer. He, Satan, the believer's enemy, will be destroyed in the end!

THE VICTORY IS THE LORD'S (REVELATION 20)!

• Satan will be bound

Then I saw an angel coming down from heaven,
holding in his hand the key to the bottomless pit
and a great chain. And he seized the dragon, that
ancient serpent, who is the devil and Satan, and
bound him for a thousand years.

— Revelation 20:1–2

• Satan will be imprisoned

And he seized the dragon, that ancient serpent, who
is the devil and Satan, and bound him for a thousand years, and threw him into the pit, and shut it
and sealed it over him, so that he might not deceive
the nations any longer, until the thousand years were

- The saints will reign

Then I saw thrones, and seated on them were those
to whom the authority to judge was committed.
Also, I saw the souls of those who had been behead-
ed for the testimony of Jesus and for the word of
God, and those who had not worshiped the beast
or its image and had not received its mark on their
foreheads or their hands. They came to life and
reigned with Christ for a thousand years.

— Revelation 20:4

- The great resurrection

The rest of the dead did not come to life until the
thousand years were ended. This is the first resurrection. Blessed and holy is the one who shares in the
first resurrection! Over such the second death has no
power, but they will be priests of God and of Christ,
and they will reign with him for a thousand years.

— Revelation 20:5–6

And when the thousand years are ended, Satan will be released from his prison and will come out to deceive the nations that are at the four corners of the earth, Gog and Magog, to gather them for battle; their number is like the sand of the sea.

— Revelation 20:7–8

• The battle ends before it begins

And they marched up over the broad plain of the earth and surrounded the camp of the saints and the beloved city, but fire came down from heaven and consumed them, and the devil who had deceived them was thrown into the lake of fire and sulfur where the beast and the false prophet were, and they will be tormented day and night forever and ever.

— Revelation 20:9–10

• The white throne judgment (not for believers)

Then I saw a great white throne and him who was seated on it. From his presence the earth and sky fled away, and no place was found for them.

— Revelation 20:11

And I saw the dead, great and small, standing before the throne, and books were opened. Then another book was opened, which is the book of life. And the dead were judged by what was written in the books, according to what they had done. And the sea gave up the dead who were in it, Death and Hades gave up the dead who were in them, and they were judged, each one of them, according to what they had done.

— Revelation 20:12–13

• Death and Hades are cast into the lake of fire

Then Death and Hades were thrown into the lake of fire. This is the second death, the lake of fire. And if anyone's name was not found written in the book of life, he was thrown into the lake of fire.

— Revelation 20:14–15

THE VICTORY IS THE LORD'S!

Beloved, no matter what you're going through now or may face in the future, just hold on to the promises of God and stand firm in your faith! For the battle has already been won. Nothing is too hard for God to handle; nothing is too small for His concern; turn it all over to Him and walk in His rest and peace!

a great help to you. Even more, I pray that you will be a great help to others. May God be glorified through you and your life's journey. May the love of God fill you, His presence, surround you, His protection, cover you, as His Spirit lives in you and gives you all that you need. Go and live a life pleasing to our Father that His name may be glorified in you and through you! Amen!

· ·

In and Out of Season,
I Will Stand.
With God,
I Cannot Fail!

Stay Wrapped in His Word!

SUGGESTED WORSHIP SONG

- "My King for Forever" by Josh Baldwin

Pick your favorite songs from this study and worship and praise God for the time spent with Him over these thirty days.

To God be the glory!

If you would like to contact the author, you can reach her in the following way:

- E-mail: kimelacurtis@gmail.com
- FB Messenger: SharingintheJourneywithKimela-Curtis
- Website: www.KimelaCurtis.com

1   Easton, Matthew George. "Entry for Sanctification." "Easton's Bible Dictionary." https://biblestudytools.com/dictionaries/eastons-bible-dictionary/sanctification.html

2   CharliesNames. "Kamela—Origin, meaning, pronunciation & popularity." Accessed March 30th, 2022. https:// charlies-names.com/en/kamela/

3   CharliesNames. "Melik—Origin, meaning, pronunciation & popularity." Accessed March 30th, 2022. https://charlies-names.com/en/melik/

Printed in the USA
CPSIA information can be obtained
at www.ICGtesting.com
LVHW010913061023
760263LV00037B/777